Manners *and* Tea *with* Mrs. B

AN ENRICHMENT WORKBOOK

Special Event Tea Parties | Manners & Etiquette Training | Camps

WWW.TEAWITHMRSB.COM

Manners and Tea with Mrs. B: An Enrichment Workbook (v2)
by Rebecca Czarniecki, illustration and book design by Katie Roland

ISBN: 978-0-9863560-0-1

Printed in the U.S.A.

Special thanks to our supportive families, friends and those who have helped bring the magic of Mrs. B to life! This would have remained a dream without the guidance of Madeline Stine, Cait Czarniecki, Stephanie Chauny and *you!*

Rediscover, dust off and bring to life
good manners. They will guarantee many
wonderful surprises. Have fun coloring,
doodling, and sharing these lessons,
collected here with love and joy.

Hugs, Mrs. B.

LET YOUR GARDEN *Grow*
Everyday Manners....................................... 2

WAYS WE *Communicate*
Body Language... 4

SMILE *Big!*
Personal Connections 6

PLEASED TO *Meet* YOU!
Introductions 8

WHERE TO *Begin*
Conversations 10

Special DELIVERY
Speaking Clearly....................................... 12

THE ART *of* A COMPLIMENT
Compliments... 14

DO I *have* TO WRITE A *thank you note?*
Thank You Notes....................................... 16

ACTIVI-*teas!*
Fun Games to Doodle and Do 18

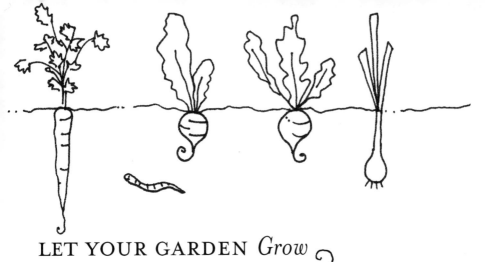

LET YOUR GARDEN *Grow*

Manners are like a garden. They need some
help to grow. Each lesson is a flower in
the garden of good manners. A seed
is planted when you learn. It grows when
you practice. As your garden blooms, so
will your confidence. Make sure to weed
out your bad habits. Good manners will
accompany you in life. Others will admire
and enjoy the beauty.

WHAT DOES YOUR
Good Manners Garden
LOOK LIKE?

☐ A JUMBLE OF UGLY WEEDS?

OR

☐ WELL KEPT AND COLORFUL?

...or a little of both?

WAYS WE *Communicate*

How do animals communicate without talking?
They use their body and eyes to say it all!
Take a playful approach to how you sit, stand,
wait, or interact with others. Do you fidget?
Chew on your clothes? Pick your nose? The
things we do on the outside show how we feel
on the inside. Learn to communicate without
saying a word.

A DOG TELLS YOU
HE IS HAPPY
BY WAGGING HIS TAIL.
FOR US, IT MEANS:

☐ SHOULDERS BACK
☐ CHIN UP
☐ SMILE ON OUR FACE
WITH *bright eyes*.

SMILE *Big!*

Everyone can smile, so practice yours!
Mrs. B uses three smiles: #1, #2, and #3.
Smiles and laughter are the same all over
the world. While you may not be able to speak
other languages, you can always communicate
with a smile or laughter. Connect your words
with a smile to make every interaction friendly.

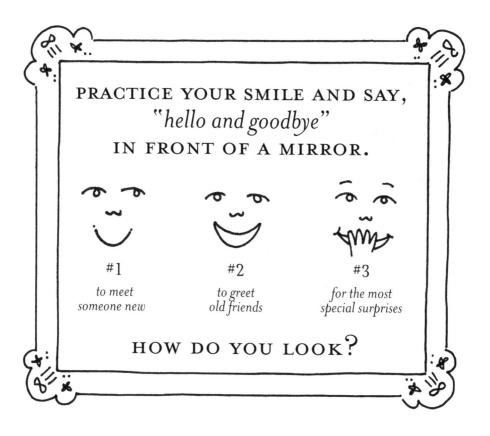

PRACTICE YOUR SMILE AND SAY,
"hello and goodbye"
IN FRONT OF A MIRROR.

#1

*to meet
someone new*

#2

*to greet
old friends*

#3

*for the most
special surprises*

HOW DO YOU LOOK?

PLEASED TO *Meet* YOU!

Everyone likes making friends. There are
five things to do when meeting someone
new. Use *Mrs. B's High-Five* of introductions.
It is not the kind of high-five you give on
the field, but it is a full-body contact sport.
It starts with your eyes and goes to your toes.
It works wherever you go. You always win with
a proper hello!

EYE CONTACT
Look directly into their eyes

MOUTH
Say something to connect, then smile

EARS
Listen to what the person says

HAND SHAKE
Make it just right... not too hard or too soft

FEET CONTACT
Point your feet toward the other person

WHERE TO *Begin*

Knowing how to make a proper introduction
is the same as adding air to tires. Creative
questions which require more than a "YES"
or "NO" answer are the fuel. Fire up your
engine and imagination for great adventures!
Listen to what others say and ask questions.
Try it out at the dinner table tonight.

Swoosh...DING!

"WHAT WAS THE
best part
OF YOUR DAY?"

Special DELIVERY

Others can hear a smile in your voice.
Sometimes it is not about what you say
but how you say it. Collect a few thoughts
before you speak. Ask yourself, "What is
the most important part?" Then, pick your
packaging. Do you prefer a gift in a paper
bag or in a beautifully wrapped box, tied
with a ribbon and bow? A clear, strong,
happy voice is a true gift.

THE ART *of* A COMPLIMENT

Giving or receiving a compliment is like a water balloon toss. Exchanging compliments lets the game continue. We want the other person to accept our compliment and respond. Sometimes a simple "thank you" will keep the game going.

TRY GIVING A COMPLIMENT
TO SOMEONE YOU WOULD
LIKE TO KNOW.

You look nice today!

Thank you!

DO I *have* TO WRITE A *thank you note?*

Yes! A real, handwritten note or letter is also a present. Writing letters, like giving gifts, takes time. Start by choosing the card. Use a special pen, maybe some stickers or fancy tape. Collect your thoughts and put it all together. *Voilà!* When writing a thank you note, you build a bridge between the giver, the gift and you. Share the joy you received from their gift!

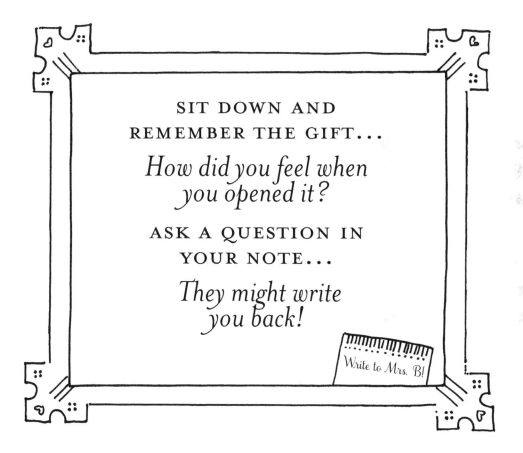

SIT DOWN AND
REMEMBER THE GIFT...

*How did you feel when
you opened it?*

ASK A QUESTION IN
YOUR NOTE...

*They might write
you back!*

Write to Mrs. B!

WORD *Scramble*

Manners

N S N A M E R

Party

A T P R Y

Teacup

P E C T A U

Surprise

I S E R P S U R

Friends

N S E D I F R

DECORATE *the* TEACUP

...add a handle and saucer too!

CONNECT *the* DOTS

FIND *the* WORDS

```
E G O N S P B D C T H U G S S
D C S U W T O H I V C H K V W
L E O H A N D S H A K E N K O
O T S M P N Y C P Z G L Y E O
V P P H M G L G A E G E S Y S
E G R I W U A M B K K T M E H
L T E G K I N R R E E T I C D
Y E S H D P G I D S W E L O I
B A E F Y M U T C E B R E N N
H P N I L I A D R A N S E T G
A O T V T K G F U N T D Z A F
P T S E R G E M K Z K I E C G
P C O M P L I M E N T S O T J
Y S W E E T H A N K Y O U N K
I N T R O D U C T I O N S F D
```

BODY LANGUAGE	HANDSHAKE	MRS.B
CAKE	HAPPY	PRESENTS
COMMUNICATION	HIGH FIVE	SMILE
COMPLIMENTS	HUGS	SWEET
EYECONTACT	INTRODUCTIONS	SWOOSHDING
FUN	LETTERS	TEAPOT
GARDEN	LOVELY	THANK YOU

Good manners are treasures to keep close.
Bring them out for the smallest occasion.
Kind thoughts and actions matter the most,
for life is a celebration.

48339627R00017

Made in the USA
Middletown, DE
15 September 2017